CW01052126

Dingoes and Marsupial Lions

David Chan

Wizard Publishing

Copyright © 2007 by David Chan

The right of David Chan to be identified as the Author of the Work has been asserted by him in accordance with the Copyright, Design and Patents Act 1988

First published in Great Britain by Wizard Publishing in 2007

All rights reserved. No part of this publication may be reproduced, stored in a retrieval system, or transmitted in any form or by other means without the written permission of the publishers, nor be otherwise circulated in any form of binding, cover or sleeve other than that in which it is published and without similar conditions being imposed on the subsequent purchaser

ISBN 9780955021015

The Author and Publishers have made all reasonable efforts to clarify ownership of quoted content and copyright and have acknowledged accordingly. However if errors have been unintentionally made, owners are invited to contact the publishers so that acknowledgement can be given.

All illustrations are the copyright work of © Dave Stephens
Cover design by Paul Dunning

Typeset by Hope Services (Abingdon) Ltd.
Printed on acid free paper from sustainable resources by
Postscript Print & Design. Tring. UK. Tel: 01442 820910

Published By:
Wizard Publishing
17 Tovey Close
London Colney
Hertfordshire
AL2 1LF

Contents

About the Author

David Chan has been a senior executive and a management consultant working across many sectors of industry including secondments to Central Government Departments.

He has worked for several Blue-Chip organisations and has experience of large and small organisations in both the public and private sector. He has been the Honorary Fellow in Information Management at Bradford University and has also been a board-level director with a subsidiary of a FTSE 150 company.

David has interests in a wide number of areas including management, business, technology, evolution and complex adaptive systems. He lives in Hertfordshire with two cats. He also enjoys playing bridge online, creative writing, songwriting and can be found sometimes performing at local folk clubs.

Acknowledgements

I would like to thank Tim Channon and members of ecademy who read the initial drafts of the book and made great suggestions. I would also like to acknowledge Gilbert Massara, the publisher, without whose support this project would have languished on a computer drive. Also I would like to express my appreciation of Alison Renshaw in her role as editor who has pruned the worst excesses of my language and has also been invaluable in seeking out references for those I have quoted.

David Chan
St Albans
2007

Author's Preface

Don't you just love Science? Just when you think you have things worked out, someone comes along with information that destroys your pet theory. When Wegener came up with the observation that the continents seem to fit together, geologists and geographers dismissed his ideas. Now we all accept plate tectonics as an accepted explanation of geological phenomena.

When I started writing this book I was searching for a biological analogy that would fit what I was saying about the changing competitive landscape. I had seen a television programme about the extinction of the large marsupial carnivores, so I thought the use of Dingoes and Marsupial Lions would be a good graphic analogy. To my horror, I learnt that the most recent genetic research would suggest that the Dingo was only five-and-a-half thousand years old and could not, therefore, have contributed to the demise of the old Marsupial Lions! I seriously thought about changing the analogy to some other competing species. However, by now I had got used to using the term 'Dingo Organisation' so

I decided to leave the original exposition in the book and address this slight factual inaccuracy in the author's preface.

I recalled reading the book, "The Science of Diskworld" by Terry Pratchett and Ian Stewart. In the book they explained that the science we were taught at school was not exactly correct but was correct enough to help us understand what was being taught at that stage; as we progressed in the subject adjustments to our simplified learning could help us grasp the more 'correct' and complex theories later on. With this caveat in mind, I decided to retain the Dingo analogy as it is perfect for the introduction of my topic to you. It has nothing to do with the fact that I find the dingo a cute dog. Really!

The dingo started to compete with
the marsupial lion . . .

1

Dingoes and Marsupial Lions

Introduction

Some 60,000 years ago, the top predator on the Australian continent was a species called the marsupial lion. This animal was the size of a leopard but was a marsupial like the kangaroo or koala. It was the top of the food chain. Nothing hunted it but it could hunt and feed on anything.

About 50,000 years ago, Homo sapiens arrived on the continent bringing with them domestic animals such as the dog. Some of these dogs became feral. The humans started to transform the landscape through using fire, changing the ecological balance of the environment. Some of the feral dogs died but some adapted to this new environment and evolved into the species we know as the dingo. The dingo started to compete with the marsupial lions and eventually displaced it as the top predator (apart from man, that is). The last marsupial lion was believed to have died about 13,000 years ago.

What is the point of this story? The first point is that the dingoes won not because they were bigger or more aggressive but through the operation of small advantages working over a long time scale. The two predators coexisted for 33,000 years. The second point is that the species that adapts better to the changes in environment eventually displaces the other.

Before we explore this analogy further, let us look at the organisations that we have at present. Our model of organisation is that of a 'command and control' hierarchy. We all accept that organisations must have a board or steering committee who are responsible for achieving an organisations' objectives (ref: Sarbanes and Oxley legislation[1]).We also believe that this group should be responsible for the organisation delivering to its objectives.

In our market economies we allow such organisations to form in order to deliver goods and services that enhance our lives. Through the operation of the market, we allow shareholders to invest in these organisations for a return on investment (basically a rent for money). Through limited liability and the stock market, we allow these organisations to separate ownership from management. We hope that 'free markets' will ensure the delivery of goods and services at an optimum price, and, products are supplied that are needed. However, we know markets are imperfect and very few are free. There is also a significant

[1] The Sarbanes and Oxley Act 2002 was legislation introduced in the US as a result of some well publicised corporate scandals such as the Enron case. Under this act, directors of public companies became liable for all aspects of the company's activities whereas before, they only had to show that they took reasonable care.

imbalance in power between the supplier and the consumer, particularly in information.

Large organisations have much more informational power than consumers. For example, if you were to purchase support services for utilities or IT support, it would be very difficult to find information on the support performance of the organisation; such as, average response times to calls, average fix times etc. Further, the service agreements often say little more than the supplier company will provide support at 'best endeavours'.

An example of this is the HomeCare Plans for central heating and boiler maintenance offered by British Gas. If you look at the contracts, there are no undertakings regarding how quickly they respond to a call or how quickly they guarantee to fix a fault.

With the success of such hierarchic organisations in the private sector, we have begun to adopt similar structures in the public sector. In the UK, the last two decades of the 20th Century saw public sector organisations adopting some of the language, if not the practices, of the commercial command and control organisations. Public sector projects are now judged on criteria based on financial returns. The worship of commercial practices has also resulted in the introduction of public and private partnerships where private sector funding is used to finance public services.

Hierarchies tend to view their customers as assets to be exploited. Read any marketing text and you will see exhortations asking companies to cross-sell products and maximise the yield from customers. In public sector organisations customers are not the prime focus of managerial attention. Customers are a distraction from trying to achieve targets set by government. Delivering customer satisfaction and value to the customer rarely gets a look in. If the senior group of management views customers as assets to be exploited or as an annoying distraction, what is likely to be this group's attitude to its employees?

The traditional organisation arranged under hierarchic lines was probably necessary because the socio-technical systems for delivering goods and services needed such entities in the past. Just like the feudal system was appropriate in building kingdoms before the modern era, the command and control hierarchy may have been necessary to exploit the opportunities from mass production and industrialisation.

Let us get back to dingoes and marsupial lions. I believe the traditional organisation is analogous to the marsupial lion. Globalisation and technology are changing the environment for organisations. The marsupial lions may have started noticing that the landscape was changing and were probably trying to adapt. The question I pose is 'where are the Dingoes?'.

This book is about one approach to building a profitable business based on another way of looking at the relationship between a business and its customers. I am hoping the businesses that I describe will become the Dingoes and, over time, out-compete the current organisations and hence dominate the business landscape.

THE MARSUPIAL LION

Before we look at this new type of organisation, let's have a closer look at our old friend, the command and control hierarchic organisation. I do not know the derivation of this statement but I first read it in **Terry Pratchett's "Maskerade"**.

"The kicking and punching stopped only when it became apparent that all the mob was attacking was itself. And, since the IQ of a mob is the IQ of its most stupid member divided by the number of mobsters, it was never very clear to anyone what had happened.[2]

I believe it can also apply to the traditional organisation but perhaps modified to something like

The IQ of an organisation is the IQ of the Chief Executive divided by the number of people in the organisation – (The IQ Rule)

It is not exactly true but you can see my point. How often have you seen people's creativity stifled within large organisations? How often do you see the politically savvy employee getting promoted ahead of the competent ones? Large organisations often pay lip service to empowerment, customer focus et al, yet most employees know only 'self-motivated yes-men' get promoted. You may be good at the job but unless you have the organisational political skills, you just won't get on once you get to the glass ceiling that separates middle management from senior management. The opposite does not hold. In many organisations, having the organisational political skills is all you need to get on.

Why does this happen? I believe I have an explanation. I cannot prove it but it seems a reasonable argument so I will rehearse it here.

Large organisations become political hierarchies because of monopoly power. Monopoly power can be expressed as dominating a particular sector or niche in the market place. For example, Microsoft has had a virtual monopoly on the desktop PC operating systems market for almost a quarter of a century. An organisation may have monopoly power even if it does not dominate a market niche. Where an organisation is part of an oligopoly (a small number of companies dominating a market

---

[2] From Maskerade by Terry Pratchett, published by Corgi. Reprinted by permission of The Random House Group Ltd.

The IQ Rule . . .

niche, e.g. retail clearing banks in the UK) and where there is little incentive to upset the status quo, then such organisations have virtual monopoly power over their customers. Another area of monopoly power is in the public sector. I have little choice over schooling in my locale in the UK. I cannot really do much if I am dissatisfied with the Driver and Vehicle licensing Agency (DVLA) or the Passport Agency in the UK.

Monopolies do not have to care about their customers nor worry about competitors. Pick up any book on strategic marketing or business strategy and they will exhort the organisation to dominate a segment of the market. Even branding is about trying to create customer loyalty and hence a virtual monopoly. In other words, creating a mini-monopoly is the objective of most business strategies. If you have dominance, then you can exploit your market position more effectively.

Now look at the implied world view. Commercial organisations become large because they enjoy monopolistic power over a segment of the market. This leads to viewing customers as assets to be exploited. If senior management view customers as assets to be exploited, isn't that likely to carry over to how it views their employees? In this way, commercial organisations actually become stupid. They will exploit the customer and will not see lower-level employees as sources of ideas and innovation. All they want from employees, who are most likely to be closest to the customer, is compliance with orders from above.

In the public sector it gets much worse. If I don't like the way the government handles my passport renewal, what real power do I have to change it? If I am not happy with the local state hospital or state school, the only thing I can do is to run a campaign and get others on board. I might make a difference in three to five years, if I am lucky.

People who run public sector organisations know full well that delivering satisfaction to their customers is not the real agenda. The real agenda is to satisfy the political demands while keeping within the legal constraints and hoping that they won't do too much to upset their end-customers. Again, such organisations will satisfy the IQ rule.

So the traditional hierarchic organisation dominates the business landscape. It has been extremely successful in the past and is the model of organisation that we know and recognise. However, I believe such organisations can be likened to the marsupial lion in Australia of 50,000 years ago. But, the landscape is changing and the Dingoes are evolving.

The following chapter looks at this changing landscape, explores the implications of the Law of Increasing Returns, and proposes the design of the new Dingo organisation.

KEY INSIGHTS

- Traditional command and control hierarchies dominate our business landscape
- Change in the business environment is altering the landscape
- Traditional companies in monopolistic positions are 'exploitative' of customers and employees. There must be a better way!

2

Emerging Landscape

Much has been written about the digital revolution and globalisation of the world economy. I will not rehash what has been written but I shall, in this chapter, highlight some of the factors that will be relevant to the emergence of *Dingoes.*

For about the last seven years, I have regularly played bridge on the Internet. This is a four person card game that is quite complicated to learn but immensely enjoyable to play. Before the Internet, you played bridge by organising at least four people to go to a venue or attend a bridge club. With the Internet, when I want to play bridge, I can log onto any of a number of games sites at any time and find people with whom I can play. I am no longer restricted by geography or time. I can also play Chess, Go, and almost any game I want online. Recently, Internet poker has become a huge business and even the traditional Poker organisers are allowing Internet tournament winners as qualifiers to their main events. It may soon be possible that an Internet qualifier may win a World Poker Tour (WPT) **Champion's** bracelet!

Similarly, there has been a growth in Internet dating sites. Many mature single people are finding that the Internet dating sites are the only way that they can meet people of a similar age and who have similar interests. From something that was seen as rather pathetic and perhaps seedy, Internet dating has become socially acceptable.

Although Internet dating is about making a one-on-one relationship, there are a large minority of members who do not want to date in the traditional sense. Some members seem willing to pay the high membership fees to extend their social network. A friend of mine actually organises monthly lunches for people on an online dating site so that people can meet in groups without the pressure of one-on-one dating. I suspect the owners of the dating site do not know that she is doing this.

I have an inkjet printer. The last set of ink cartridges I bought were not from a local shop. Instead, I went onto Google and searched for the best prices. I saved about 30% off the local shop prices by purchasing from a retailer operating from France. I paid using a credit card and the cartridges were delivered in three days. The retailer also provided me with a facility to track the order. The goods were shipped from a warehouse outside Paris to a distribution point in Utrecht and then flown to England.

Very recently, I was invited to stay with some friends on the Costa del Sol. I used the Internet to find the cheapest flight, booked the parking at the UK airport, and booked the hire car at Malaga Airport.

All this change means that there are opportunities now that have not occurred before. In the past, we have only interacted with people that we have met face-to-face. With these changes, we have ways of interacting with others electronically through the Internet. Using the Internet, it is easy to find people who have the same interests as you and to interact with them through email, bulletin boards and interactive chat. Even if your interests are esoteric, it is likely you will find some Internet forum or website that will cater for this. This brings the possibility of new types of communities where people interact electronically. I will use the term Communities of Interest (CoIs) in this book for communities that interact virtually through digital media. CoIs represent a major business opportunity.

The business landscape is changing rapidly. The factors that are relevant to this discussion on business organisation are:-
• The world is digitally connected
• The Internet spans countries and disregards geographical distances
• It enables like-minded people to interact
• It is distributed not centralised
• It cannot be controlled
• It is not naturally monopolistic

This is analogous to environments changing in the natural world. With changes in the natural environment, there are new opportunities for species. Australia 50,000 years ago was a lot more forested than it is now. It is believed that when the ancestors of the aborigines arrived in Australia, they changed the landscape through slash and burn agricultural techniques. Over the last 50 millennia the environment of the continent has been transformed. Although the marsupial lions were the top predators, they gradually died out and became extinct 37,000 years later!

One of the largest 'marsupial lions' is the Microsoft Corporation.

It dominates the desktop market place and its operating systems are used by most PCs across the planet. Its main challenger is not another marsupial lion organisation but a consortium of volunteers: the Linux community. The rise of the Linux operating system and the emergence of Open Source software are well documented and can be read on the website for the Open Source organisation. However, community-based groupings are causing the Marsupial Lions to behave differently. The following story illustrates this.

My son is passionate about the Welsh language. Although our family has no direct connection with Wales (apart from both he and I have Christian names after the Welsh patron Saint), he decided to study Welsh GCSE while he was doing his undergraduate and Masters Degrees. He then went on to do an A Level in Welsh when he started work as a software engineer. He and a few Welsh language enthusiasts asked Microsoft in 2003 whether they could have a version of Microsoft Office in the Welsh language. Microsoft replied that there were no plans to deliver a Welsh version as the market base was so small.

Not deterred by this, my son then worked with a number of Welsh speaking volunteers to create a version of OpenOffice, the Open Source free equivalent of Microsoft Office. At the 2004 Eisteddfod in Newport, they announced to the Welsh language media that an early version of OpenOffice was available for distribution. Straight away, Microsoft announced that a Welsh language version would be available in nine months.

The point here is that a small group of dedicated people can affect the behaviour of a large corporation. Decision cycles and product life-cycles are shortening. Smaller competitors can have a large effect on established organisations. In just such a way the marsupial lions had to contend with competing dingoes some

... dedicated people can affect
the behaviour of large corporations ...

fifty thousand years ago. Without the dingo the marsupial lion was the undisputed top predator in the food chain. Once the dingo arrived the marsupial lion had competition and had to start adjusting to the new realities.

In the next chapter we will look at one of the new opportunities created by technology and see how Digital technology can turn the Law of Diminishing Returns on its head!

KEY INSIGHTS

- The business landscape is changing rapidly under the force of globalisation and technological change
- Smaller groups and organisations are beginning to have an affect on the strategies and plans of large established organisations
- The pace of change is increasing

3

Law of Increasing Returns

Most people will be familiar with the Law of Diminishing Returns. This law says that as production expands, there will come a point when the cost of producing an additional unit of output will increase. If we sell each unit of output at a certain price, as we increase production, the returns will diminish.

This makes sense if we are producing widgets in a factory. At some point our production lines will be running at full capacity. To increase production, we may have to go to overtime working or even put on a night shift. Both of these add to the unit labour costs. When we reach the factory's capacity, we will have to buy a new factory with additional set-up costs all decreasing the returns on each unit. Producing more and more output may require us to build another factory and yet another. Ultimately, we will find that co-ordinating production across several factories would prove increasingly difficult and costly.

Similarly, if we have a business based upon a sequence of manual processes, such as new customer processing in banking or passport applications, we would still be subject to the Law of Diminishing Returns. With a certain set of systems and levels of staffing we might be able to cope with extra volumes, by asking staff to work overtime or putting on additional shifts. Once again, if this maximum capacity is reached, then we would have to employ more staff (which might require additional office space and equipment) or set up an additional processing centre.

This is the Law of Diminishing Returns and it applied to most organisations throughout the industrial age. Whether it is manufacturing, agriculture, retailing or any of the businesses that handle physical goods or need physical resources (people and things), this law seems to apply. Although we can improve efficiency by adopting new methods (this is what is called business process redesign), we always seem to come up against the Law of Diminishing Returns.

In some senses, the IQ Rule proposed in chapter one is a restatement or corollary of the Law of Diminishing Returns. What we are saying is, as the number of people in an organisation increases, the complexity required to control these people increases accordingly. Therefore, more and more of the CEO's attention must be focused on controlling the organisation. This is a result from Control Theory. If this sort of thing interests you, read up Ashby's 'Law of Requisite Variety'[3].

In total contrast, when we look at the digital world, the Law of Diminishing Returns can be turned on its head. In the digital world, software, pictures, text, images, sound and movies exist as digits on a server somewhere. If these are available on the

[3] Ashby, W. R. (1958). Requisite variety and its implications for the control of complex systems. In George J. Klir (1991), Facets of systems science.

Internet, then anyone can access these if they too have access to the Internet.

Now let us look at the costs incurred by the supplier of digital media. The supplier has to create the file (this might be a very large cost if it is software or media rich content). There is the cost of distribution which is the costs incurred by the supplier in connecting to the Internet (this is actually quite low). Finally there is the unit cost of an extra copy of the file.

What is the real cost of producing another copy piece of software or media content across the Internet? The answer is that it costs practically nothing! Hosting costs for plugging your site into the Internet start from about £120 per year. You can run high traffic site for £5,000 per year. Next time you buy software or download entertainment from the Internet, remember it costs the supplier practically nothing. In fact, once the original costs of producing the digital content have been recovered, the revenue is practically all profit. The only expenditure for the supplier is the cost of keeping a server attached to the Internet and the advertising and promotion to get you to download it!

This is the **Law of Increasing Returns** In the digital world the cost of an additional unit tends towards zero. Once you have recovered your original development costs and you have plenty of capacity on your servers, the revenue from each additional sale is practically all profit.

"Increasing Returns and Path Dependence in the Economy" is the title of a book by Brian Arthur[4]. It describes the conditions that allow organisations to gain an overwhelming advantage in the marketplace. It is an interesting read for anyone who wants to understand how products can become dominant in a particular marketplace.

[4] Ann Arbor, University of Michigan Press, 1994

Our normal thinking about organisations and buying is based upon what has worked in the Industrial Revolution. We have been conditioned to think that we have to pay the same price for each transaction. We also think it is fair to pay the suppliers their asking price. Indeed our institutions that monitor and regulate markets work on principles that are based upon enabling organisations that have to work under the Law of Diminishing Returns.

A good example of this is the thorny issue of Software Patents. In the USA, a company can patent a business process that is encapsulated in software. An analogy will illustrate what this means. Let's go back in history and pretend that the only way of fishing known is to spear the fish with a spear or a harpoon. Some bright spark invents the fishing net which allows greater efficiency in fishing. If the system of current software patents applied to the fishing methods of our analogy, then a patentor could patent the fishing net and anyone using the net technique or any supplier of fishing nets would have to pay a royalty to the patentor!

Legislation to enable Software Patents was presented to the EU Parliament in summer 2005. The larger software firms such as Microsoft and Oracle lobbied Members of the European Parliament ("MEPs") intensively in favour of this and three months before the vote, it looked like being carried. Then, a consortium of volunteers working in the Open Source community started their own lobbying efforts with MEPs and managed to defeat the motion, arguing that the present copyright laws provided reasonable protection and that granting software patents would allow large companies to create too much monopoly power. To date, *the only legislation that allows Software Patents is the US.* Software Patents show how even governments might be seduced by the arguments of big, wealthy companies and legislate to improve these companies' monopoly power.

Very recently, a patent law firm in America asked the US Courts to allow storyline plots to be patented. This would allow an author to patent the structure of a plot line. If any other authors, playwrights or screenplay writers use the basic plots, they would have to pay a royalty to the holder of a patent.

Another example of the potential opportunities presented by the Law of Increasing Returns is illustrated by a project in which I was involved. In 1994, I was the Chairman of the Alumni Association of the Management Centre, University of Bradford. We were looking at ways to raise the profile of the Management Centre, raise additional revenues for the Association and promote the notion of post-graduate management education to the public at large. We decided to do this through running a management game based on a computer simulation.

We persuaded some of the academics to help us specify a strategic management simulation and found a games author who was prepared to build it for us at very little cost. We persuaded Hewlett Packard to donate £20,000 worth of equipment as a prize. We also persuaded several sponsors to work with us donating their products and services free. Thus the Venture business game was born. We had advertising sponsors who were prepared to give us space and an accountancy magazine wrote monthly editorials on the progress of the game.

We had costed out that a charge of £250 per team would allow us to break even if we got ten teams to play, although we were secretly hoping to have twenty teams. Within the first week of publishing the game we had the twenty teams registered. By the time we ran the game, we had eighty-two teams playing the game. Since the game was based on a computer simulation, the additional effort required to run more than twenty teams was trivial and the additional profits went straight into the Alumni Association's account.

The Law of Increasing Returns provides
opportunities . . .

If we can build a business that can take advantage of the Law of Increasing Returns and which is not a power hierarchy, then we may be on the way to describing the Dingo that may eventually replace the marsupial lion.

KEY INSIGHTS

- In the Industrial Age where products and services relied upon physical goods and human input, the Law of Diminishing Returns applied across the marketplace
- In the Post-Industrial Age where products and services are informational based and primarily digitised a different law, The Law of Increasing Returns applies.
- Our current thinking, our institutions and our power structures are designed to support organisations that deliver their output under the Law of Diminishing Returns
- The Law of Increasing Returns provides opportunities for potential Dingo organisations to evolve.

"Elephants must learn to dance" . . .

4

Opportunities

I worked on a strategy study covering the future of Broadcasting in the Digital Age while I was at the BBC in the late 1990s. One phrase in the final presentation stuck in my mind. It was constructed to illustrate the necessity for large media corporations to adapt flexibly with changing technology. The phrase we used was, "Elephants must learn to dance". If what I have said in the previous chapter is correct then elephants can't learn to dance. Furthermore, if the business and competitive landscape is changing as rapidly as I think, there will be new niches available simply because the elephants will be falling over as they try to tango.

Why should this be so? The IQ rule gives us one reason why the marsupial lions may not adapt. There are other reasons based around the cultural attitudes and behaviours reinforced by the way the traditional businesses are funded and managed. I shall take a brief detour to explore these reasons.

Suppose we want to start a traditional business. It may be in manufacturing or in services. The first thing we would have to do is to find some premises in which to work, buy any equipment we may need, advertise or promote our company, employ and train staff and start production. We may even need to fund the business through a period before our revenues cover our costs. This all takes money.

Unless you have the funds yourself, you would need to borrow from banks or from investors such as Business Angels or Venture Capitalists. All investors want to minimise their risks and the best way to do that is to ensure that the money is paid back as quickly as possible whether in cash or in sales of share. Therefore, when you start a business you have pressure from investors to drive the business as hard as possible. This means that you will start viewing your customers as sources of profits and assets to be exploited.

Let us now look at the position of the directors of a company that is a going concern that is either a subsidiary of a quoted company or a quoted company itself. Directors of a quoted company are required to deliver the results expected by the investors. Woe betide you if you deliver profit below the market's expectations. The consequence of consistently failing to deliver market expectations is that you lose your job!

Therefore, for people running traditional companies, there is always the pressure to maximise the profits and to take a short term view. Although many boardrooms pay lip service to slogans like, "Customer First" or "Quality Service", the reality is that customers are viewed as assets to be exploited.

In the last two decades it was quite fashionable for large organisations to run culture-change programmes that aligned/ realigned their business processes to deliver improved quality to their customers. Often these were combined with programmes of employee empowerment where the hierarchy was to be inverted and customer-facing employees were empowered to make decisions that would enable them to deliver good service to their customers. Front-line staff were to be backed up by an internal team dedicated to providing improved quality to their customers. However, few programmes achieved anything like their expected outcomes since much of this, however well intentioned, was just 'window dressing' as few hierarchic organisations could genuinely empower their front line staff. Sadly Rule 1 operates.

A few years ago, I happened to be in the processing centre for a major clearing bank talking to some of the staff. Plastered across all the walls were posters and slogans such as "Our objective is to deliver satisfaction to our customers", "We are a team dedicated to providing a quality service", or, "There is no I in Team!" I asked one of the administrators about her attitude to all this. She replied that it was all really hot air and the bosses were more concerned about meeting their own bonus targets than implementing improvements to customer services.

There is an old joke doing the rounds which goes like this. "We work in a mushroom organisation. We are kept in the dark and, regularly, our boss throws a bucket of horse dung over us". Most people who work in traditional organisations smile wryly at this.

Sadly, I am of the opinion that all such exhortations to improve customer satisfaction will have little long-term effect in traditional organisations. When the board is under pressure to maximise short-term financial performance and is distant from its customers, it will inevitably view customer service as a constraint rather than a target. In traditional organisations, the *actual* culture will flow from how the board behaves.

So, to reiterate, one of the key characteristics of the Marsupial Lion organisation is that its customers are viewed as assets to be exploited rather than a community to be served.

The last decade of the twentieth century saw a boom in Internet businesses. Venture capitalists were almost desperate to invest in a Dot Com company. We saw companies being valued at multiples of their sales even though these businesses were loss making.

Many of these start-up companies were just bad ideas that would never have worked. Some others might have become flourishing businesses if there wasn't pressure from venture capitalists to obtain quick returns. High start-up costs necessitated entre-preneurs to obtain funding from *business angels and venture capitalists*. Investors wanted high and quick returns.

In those days, none would invest in a company that proposed using Open Source software. Instead, the investors' technology advisers would insist on proprietary infrastructures that inflated the costs of building an Internet site. Yet Open Source software runs 95% of the Internet.

Today, the technology costs on start-up are a lot lower. I can host 5Gbytes of storage for a year using a Linux, Perl, PHP, MySQL infrastructure for less than £120 per year. Note, there are no software licensing costs based on volume using Open Sourced software. We also have access to services such as WorldPay, Netbank and PayPal that will allow us to take payments.

During the last decade, the cost of building an interactive site *for a business* was in the hundred thousands if not millions. Now, the cost of building interactive sites is in thousands and tens of thousands. This lowers the start-up costs significantly and avoids the pressure of venture capitalists.

This also provides another opportunity for the potential entrepreneur. If start-up costs can be lowered by an order of magnitude, then the pressure and power exerted by investors who demand a quick return is correspondingly less. Without the pressure to obtain quick returns on investments, businesses can grow at a 'natural' rate rather than being forced into artificial time scales to satisfy the needs of external investors. If a business can grow consistently at a small rate, eventually, it will reach a significant size. I call this 'The Snowball Theory of Growth'.

Let us now look at the business opportunities that are being created by globalisation and digital technology. To do this, I will take a historical detour to make some key points about organisations.

The first organisation that was important to the human race was probably the extended family. By co-operating with our kin group, we could get by in gathering, hunting, herding and subsistence farming. Such organisations probably yielded very small food surpluses and probably the largest conglomeration that these technologies could support would be the tribe of at most, a hundred people.

When agriculture became more efficient and the surpluses became sufficient to support larger populations, we see the beginning of the City State and the beginnings of formal organisations based on the power of royalty or gods. As City States became richer, they became more attractive to those who would plunder their gathering wealth and this reinforced the power of the elite groups, as the need arose to establish a standing army to protect that wealth. Elite groups perpetuated themselves through strict rules of inheritance and as a consequence the differentiation between nobles and commoners evolved, becoming an accepted part of societal infrastructures.

For much of recorded history, the ruling elites in most civilisations were the nobility who maintained power through the control of land. The agricultural revolution in eighteenth-century Europe saw a significant increase in agricultural production. This boom enabled industrialisation in the following centuries. Industrialisation produced improvements in tools, techniques and knowledge which were then fed back into agriculture leading to further agricultural efficiency. In the early 20th century, the invention of mass production led to the expansion of the professionally managed business organisation and reinforced the separation between management and ownership.

There is nothing special about a particular type of organisation and there is no such thing as a perfect organisational structure. Particular types of organisations would appear to thrive in certain types of environment. *It all depends on the circumstances and situation.* It was probably necessary to have Guilds to control production in the Medieval Times. It was probably necessary to allow monopolies in trade at particular stages in History. The Roman Empire ran all silver production as a monopoly. The British Crown granted Patents over specific areas of commerce to monopolist and oligopolies. It would probably be nonsensical to create that sort of organisation now to control manufacturing in the 21st century. As previously said, we probably needed the hierarchic organisation in the industrial era. Whether they are relevant in the post-industrial society is an open question in my mind.

I am not sure whether these figures are absolutely accurate but they will illustrate an important point. In the first City States, up to 95% of the population worked in agriculture. In the west, by the early 20th century, 50% of the population worked in agriculture. By 1950 this figure is down to 20% and now it is 3%. In the 19th century 80% of the population worked in manufacturing or agriculture and the rest in services. According to the 2001 census,

What activates the society values changes over time . . .

less than 10% of the UK working population worked in manu-facturing or agriculture sectors.

What is the significance of these statistics?

The first point is that agricultural surpluses provide opportunities to do other things. The more people a farmer can feed, the more people can devote their lives to other activities. What activities the society values changes over time. Film stars and leading sportsmen are highly valued by our society. We pay them more. David Beckham's annual earnings are about the same as the Civil List payments to the Queen. Would an athlete or a troubadour earn as much as a king in the Middle Ages?

George Gershwin, a famous popular song writer in the early twentieth century approached Igor Stravinsky, the renowned classical composer, for lessons in composition. Igor Stravinsky said to Gershwin that considering their relative annual earnings, perhaps Stravinsky should be the one taking lessons from Gershwin!

The second point is the highest growth industries presently seem to be those that engage people's interest. The computer gaming industry is growing significantly. More people are playing the most popular computer games than those watching the most popular feature films. Major businesses are being built around people's obsession with sport. People's interest in celebrities has spawned numerous magazines that report on their activities. In the UK, most tabloid newspapers carry more column inches on the latest reality TV programmes and celebrities' affairs than on news and current affairs.

As a result, I believe that Communities of Interests (CoIs) will be the biggest growth area in the future. As we grow richer, we will have more time to indulge our interests and we will naturally want to get together with those who share the same passions. Each of us will dip into different communities that meet our needs at different times. We will also pay to do so if we receive value. CoIs are just groups of people that share a common interest and that interact together to pursue this interest.

Those businesses that enable CoIs, that serve the CoIs and, that delight members of CoIs will be rewarded with profits and be defended from competitors. To successfully serve a community the serving organisation cannot view members of that community as assets to be exploited but must work with the community according to a different set of values from those of the traditional organisation.

Let's go back to the dingo. When the first dogs became feral in Australia, they did not immediately drive out the marsupial lions. I suspect isolated populations gained a foothold in a particular area and gradually expanded. The dingo became successful through the operation of small advantages over a long time scale.

Low start-up costs and opportunities created by the changing business landscape present opportunities for new types of business and business organisations to establish themselves and grow.

The next chapter looks at how we can exploit these opportunities through creating a Dingo business.

KEY INSIGHTS

- Traditional organisations view their customers as assets to be exploited and we accept this because it has always been so
- The post-industrial society provides new business niches and opportunities
- Serving Communities of Interest may well be the opportunity to build Dingo organisations

5

Building a Dingo

Given the opportunities, how does one go about building such a business? This chapter attempts to answer this question and lay down some broad principles of how a Dingo business can be built and grown. I am not setting this down as a theoretical exercise. My business partner and I, Peter Blue, are attempting to build Dingo businesses based on these principles. The following 'recipe' is not rocket science. It is just applying business-planning principles to new opportunities.

IDENTIFY YOUR COMMUNITY

The first step to creating a Dingo business is to identify a community that could be formed using the Internet and Digital technology. Each online gaming site and each online dating site is forming a nexus around which a community can grow. If you have a passion for something, these are the first areas in which to look. Alternatively, perhaps you have knowledge of a specific area of interest. For example, the founder of Betfair.com was interested in gambling and worked in the stock market. This site does not act as an online bookmaker. It matches people who offer odds on the same event and makes a charge for providing the service thereby providing a saving of about 20% against bookmakers' quotes. A success based on the identification of a Community of Interest.

The first place to start is to look at your own interests and passions. Are you a fan of a particular team, group or artist? Do you have a hobby or interest that is bordering on a passion for you? Are there others who share the same interests? Would you like to interact with people who share those interests? Are there better ways of doing this than are currently available?

If this does not work, then look at your own experiences. Is there something that you need that is difficult to get? Are there services that you would like to have readily available that are difficult to find? Do you have knowledge of some area where a service provider is not performing well?

For example, my business partner and I came across the opportunity for a rare books community **www.rarelist.co.uk** because of my passion and interest in CoIs. I was talking to a bookseller who specialised in first editions and she complained that the Internet site she used was failing her and other small-scale booksellers. When she explained that most sites charged both a monthly listing fee and up to 16% commission on each sale, I realised there was an opportunity here.

Talking to my business partner, Peter Blue, I estimated that we could create an Internet site building on the software that we already had for as little as 30 person day's effort. Hosting for the site, together with domain name registration, would cost us less than £150 per year. The site would be capable of listing 50,000 books. Given the low investment, we decided to go ahead.

Identify the target C of I

So if you are looking to start a Dingo business, start by looking at those areas that you have knowledge of or an interest in. Perhaps you know something about a particular area, or, like us, you have identified a supplier failing a group of people.

LOOK AT THE COMPETITION

Having identified the target CoI, you should then look at how this community is served by existing providers. Are there any weaknesses in their offerings? Do you know of any dissatisfaction with these service providers in the target community? How do these providers earn their money? What are their likely costs?

Then have a think about a proposition that could work. What are the likely costs? Can you come up with a better "value for money charging" scheme? Can you make yours better and cheaper than the competition? Can you provide better facilities and features that might justify a higher charge?

The Betfair.com example shows how someone with knowledge of gambling saw an opportunity to provide better value. Normally bookmakers add an on-cost to the odds of about 15% to 20% to cover their costs and make a profit. Betfair.com matches punters with each other and only takes a small percentage of the bet placed to cover costs. In effect, the company runs a market to match punters. Suppose I believe Manchester United will beat Chelsea and offer odds of 5 to 4. Betfair.com matches this with a Chelsea supporter who is willing to take such odds. This is like a stock exchange that will match sellers with buyers.

Let us get back to our rare books example. Having studied Internet sites that specialised in rare books we learned that the market leader in this segment had recently branched out into selling new books as well as collectable books as they had recently signed an agreement with a major chain of bookshops. Further discussions with other rare book sellers confirmed that there was general dissatisfaction with the service offered by this market leader and we found that we had an idea that could be much more useful to them.

We looked at the business model of the main players in this segment of the market place. All of them relied upon charging a monthly listing fee plus a commission on each sale. None of the sites charged the buyers a fee but relied upon the booksellers' rentals and sales commission for revenue. Several sites had links to new books sites and this would appear to be the main way of attracting customers.

Radically, we decided that we would not charge commissions on sales. Instead, we would charge a modest membership fee. We would rely on word-of-mouth rather than advertising campaigns to grow the site. Since we were launching the business without incurring debt, we could afford to operate the business with only a few paying members.

In looking at *your* area of interest, look at what businesses serve that particular community. Are there features or facilities that you might like or find useful that are not being provided by existing businesses? Is the community being overcharged to enjoy and share their interests? If so, try and design a proposition that will address the weaknesses of the present organisations.

DESIGN YOUR PROPOSITION

If none of the suppliers see their role as fostering and nurturing a community of interest, then you are in business. Even if they are adopting some of the principles of a CoI-based business, if you believe the supplier has an exploitative approach to their clients/customers, there may still be opportunities for you.

A CoI-based business has the following characteristics:-

- There is a shared interest around which the community can form (hobby, sports club, pop-band etc)
- There are means for members of the CoI to interconnect and communicate
- There are attractors for members of the CoI to remain with the business
- There are mechanisms to attract new members and grow the community
- Profit growth is based around increasing the membership rather than maximising the 'take' from each member
- The business is there for 'the long haul'

With the rare books site, we believed we could compete with the present providers through focusing on the community aspects. We were betting that building a business based upon enabling the community to interact more effectively would ultimately out-compete those providing a retailing/middleman/customer-referral service. We also believed that we could provide an infrastructure that would enable buying and selling without us taking a commission on each transaction. How did we do this?

The site, www.rarelist.com, is a membership site. Standard membership is free but requires the individual to set up an identifier and a member's profile. Standard members can see articles, read blogs and search for books. However, they cannot interact by posting their own articles or blogs, nor can they contact the seller of a book until they become a 'Silver Member'. A 'Silver Member' can see the full contact details of the seller and can interact with all other members. A 'Gold Member' has all the facilities of other grades of membership plus the ability to list their books for sale. We have set the membership monthly fees at £1 for a Silver member and £3 for a 'Gold Member'. We have also agreed not to increase subscription rates by more than 20% per annum.

We have also designed some mechanisms that may be of interest to other people building community-based businesses. We invite members to subscribe through using an Internet payment system. Since the monthly subscriptions are small values, we offer the members an option to pay credits into their membership account. So as a 'Gold Member', I may load £12 rather than pay £3 every month. This ability to record credits is important.

Any member may submit articles for publication on the site to our online editor. The member can 'sell' this article to us. If we publish the article, we will credit the member's account with an agreed sum. We have also built a growth factor by giving incentives to members to recruit others to the site. If a new member signs up after being referred by an existing member, the amount of the first credit paid by the new member is also paid into the referring member's account.

Using these devices, a member who is active in making our site grow can use the site for free. In this way, we can design propositions of value to CoI members that support business growth. Unlike traditional organisations we seek to reward members who contribute to the community and our business objectives. For example, some sites will encourage people to post reviews of books but offer no reward to the reviewer. Articles and book reviews help sites to become more highly-rated by search engines. The proposed approach provides members with a reward for increasing the value of the site. Personally, I would not write and post reviews for Amazon or such sites. I do not want to be contributing value when the businesses are maximising returns to the shareholders. Perhaps if they would offer a small fee or a discount off the next purchase. I might reconsider

Fostering and Nurturing your business . . .

FOSTERING AND NURTURING YOUR BUSINESS

Assuming you get the right business and technical help, you can build such a business at a relatively low cost. Rather than pay people full consulting and service fees, try to negotiate a discounted fee rate and offset this by giving suppliers a share of the equity. Doing this, you could start such a business for less than £3,000!

Unless you choose to buy membership through advertising and marketing, you can start the business in a small scale and grow the membership organically. Friendsreunited.com operated for the first ten years through word of mouth and referrals to become one of the biggest UK networks. You can make all administration functions accessible through an Internet browser. Initially working from home, you can avoid office and other administration costs. As your site's membership grows, you can then take on staff and acquire office space if the profits warrant them.

It is possible to 'jump start' the business through 'buying' membership. You can do this by advertising for members and offering incentives to other organisations for referring members to your site. The down-side is that this increases the pressure to make a return on your investment quickly. Here are some techniques:-

■ Advertising through paying the search engine for specific search words
■ Providing a commission to others that introduce members to you
■ Affiliating yourself to other clubs and organisations and giving these preferential membership terms
■ Offering free membership to selected groups within your community

Personally, I would prefer 'natural' organic growth with the site's membership increasing through direct referrals. However, in certain communities such as dating and business networking, achieving critical mass quickly is important to business viability.

KEY INSIGHTS

- CoI-based businesses can be started with relatively little cost
- Your own interests or your own knowledge base would be good starting points to investigate for potential business opportunities
- Digitally-based businesses can be started with modest initial costs and the operating costs can be grown in line with revenues
- You can 'seed' communities through advertising and promotion.

6

Conclusion

The last chapter looked at some ways to build profitable businesses based around fostering and nurturing CoIs. The Internet and the ubiquity of digital communication have changed the competitive landscape for most businesses. Few people have woken up to the possibilities that such changes generate.

Our thinking and our habits have been preconditioned by what has gone before. We believe that starting a business requires a lot of capital and incurs significant risk. Few people have recognised that *the conditions have changed significantly*. These changes could lead to a new perspective on business start-ups.

In World War I, the generals on both sides still had not seen the new realities of warfare arising out of modern artillery and the machine gun. Therefore, for the first five years, both sides sacrificed millions of soldiers in set-piece battles fighting a trench war on the Western Front. This was despite the lessons that The American Civil War had taught: that massed battles using modern firearms would lead to high casualties. Similarly, in World War II, the Allied general staff were totally unprepared for Blitzkrieg, mechanised warfare, practised by the Germans at the outbreak of the hostilities despite the fact that Blitzkrieg, (as used by the German High Command,) was based on the theories of an Englishman, Basil Liddell-Hart. It is interesting to note that the French and British had better tanks than the Germans at the outbreak of World War II; the root of the German success at this stage was to be found in their superior strategy and tactics!

It is a truism in military history that Generals always fight the previous war. Similarly, in business, many businessmen still see the market as it was, rather than as it is. People are still affected by the 'froth' of the 1990's Dot Com Bubble and the subsequent crash of the Internet marketplace and are reluctant to take the risk of starting Internet businesses. However, both the risk of failure, and the cost of start-up are now significantly less than in the last decade. Through the use of 'right' tactics and strategy, many of the *advantage*s of existing business organisations can be neutral-ised. Unfortunately, we do not know what the 'right' tactics are, or, what the 'right' strategies' are. However, because the start-up costs are several orders of magnitude less *(thousands rather than millions of pounds)* we may be able to see more experimentation and a larger number of attempts to start different types of business.

This is similar to what occurs in biology after mass extinctions. In biology, species inhabit niches of a specific ecology. In normal situations, it is difficult for a competing species to invade a particular ecological niche as the incumbent species will be better placed to compete. After a mass extinction, however, these niches become available and even *animals that are not perfectly adapted to a particular niche* can begin to occupy these niches and evolve to fit the requirements. In the archaeological record, we find straight after a mass extinction, the evolution of many species. This is the Theory of Punctuated Evolution as opposed to the Gradual Evolutionary proposed by Darwin. Many *new species* die off and fail to compete but new forms soon establish themselves.

Since the existing businesses will tend to 'fight the last war', there is an opportunity for new businesses with a different business model and a different ethical philosophy to become established. The digital economy is providing new niches that the existing organisations may find challenging to exploit. If you can start a business in a new niche, there may be some significant time before existing businesses can spot you as new competitor. This will give you time to become established.

If start-up costs are low, then many more businesses can be established. Like new species occupying niches, some will fail, some will have marginal success but some will be eventually successful and may come to dominate the landscape. CoI-based businesses are only one possible form. There will certainly be other types of businesses in the new landscape but CoI-based businesses can be started by potential entrepreneurs who have little capital but a lot of enthusiasm. You might be able to start one without "betting the farm"!

Clearly, there are risks but if you have a passion for the area and some knowledge, business risks can be mitigated substantially. By exploiting the economics of *Increasing Returns,* you can have a substantial cost advantage over existing businesses. Further, if you are dedicated to providing increasing value to the CoI, you will create a loyalty that traditional businesses cannot achieve. To compete with you, those competitors will have to become like you.

I remember a phrase that I first heard from Ed Straw, the brother of Jack the UK Cabinet Minister, when I worked as a management consultant at Coopers and Lybrand. He said, "We've talked about it long enough. Let's JFWDI[5]!"

KEY INSIGHTS

- CoI-based business can be started with little investment and little risk
- If you base your business on your own passions and interests you can even reduce these risks further
- You might even start them while you are still working for a Marsupial Lion organisation
- So why aren't you starting one?

---

[5] *Just 'Flipping' Well Do It or any variation that may occur to the reader.*

Postscript

Communities of Interest are not just restricted to clubs or people with the same hobbies. They can be found almost everywhere. The following paragraphs propose some possible COI.

Most people go to the supermarket weekly. The bulk of the shopping would be regular purchased items. Suppose people in a specific neighbourhood could get together and 'lump' these regular purchases together. Further suppose these could be channelled to a bulk buying operation and a distributor who can deliver locally. This is a potential Dingo business.

There are approximately 14 million households in the UK that own a dog. Dogs need kennelling when the owner goes on holiday and can be quite costly. Suppose someone creates a community where dog owners could register their dog's details and find other owners within a certain geographical neighbourhood. Further, suppose members of this community could contact each other through the Internet (and perhaps introduce their dogs to each other) with a view of dog-sitting for each other while on holiday.

This would be a valuable service and people may pay a small membership fee.

Suppose a performer or a band that is starting up can get people in the audience to become registered in their fan-club through a simple text message. At the end of each performance or gig, they could invite members of the audience to text them to be kept informed about the performer or band. Performer or bands can then text back to this fan-base using the Internet or mobile text message. If this can be done cheaply, then performers and bands who have not been signed by a label can afford to establish their own fan base. This is in essence my latest attempt to create a Dingo organisation. It is called www.eventprompt.co.uk.

Community-based Internet sites have become more prominent in the news recently. Take as two examples the purchase of Myspace by News Corp at a valuation of $580M and groups like the 'Arctic Monkeys' rising from obscurity by promoting themselves through Internet sites. This development would suggest that the ideas in this book may well be worthy of closer examination.